SCOOBY-DOO!

# The Clue in
# the Closet

by Frances Ann Ladd

Illustrated by Duendes del Sur

SCHOLASTIC INC.

It was time to sleep.
Shaggy opened
the closet to get
his pajamas.

*"Zoinks!"* he cried.
"A ghost is in the closet!"

Scooby and Shaggy
climbed into bed.
They clung to each other,
but they could not sleep.

Shaggy got a flashlight.
He slowly opened
the closet.
He shined
the flashlight in.
Then he slammed
the door.

"The ghost is still there!"
He slowly opened
the door again.
"The ghost is not moving,"
said Shaggy.

"Look!" Shaggy said.
"It is not a ghost!
It is only a blanket."

"These slippers
made the blanket
look like a ghost,"
said Shaggy.

Shaggy and Scooby
took the blanket to bed.
Then they went to sleep.